The Group Book:
Effective Skills for Cooperative Groups

By Maurice L. Phipps
And
Cindy A. Phipps

PARTICIPANT WORKBOOK

Published by BookLocker.com, Inc., Bradenton, Florida.

Printed on acid-free paper.

BookLocker.com, Inc.
2018

First Edition

DISCLAIMER

This book details the authors' personal experiences with and opinions about facilitating and working in groups. The co-author is a working school psychologist but is not licensed for private practice. The other co-author is a professor and researcher in cooperative learning.

The authors and publisher are providing this book and its contents on an "as is" basis and make no representations or warranties of any kind with respect to this book or its contents. The authors and publisher disclaim all such representations and warranties, including for example specific advice for a particular purpose. In addition, the authors and publisher do not represent or warrant that the information accessible via this book is accurate, complete or current.

Except as specifically stated in this book, neither the authors or publisher, nor any authors, contributors, or other representatives will be liable for damages arising out of or in connection with the use of this book. This is a comprehensive limitation of liability that applies to all damages of any kind, including (without limitation) compensatory; direct, indirect or consequential damages; loss of data, income or profit; loss of or damage to property and claims of third parties.

You understand that this book is not intended as a substitute for consultation with a licensed professional. Before you begin any change of your lifestyle in any way, you will consult a licensed professional to ensure that you are doing what's best for your situation.

This book provides content related to facilitation and group work topics. As such, use of this book implies your acceptance of this disclaimer.

THE GROUP BOOK:
Effective Skills for Cooperative Groups

Maurice L. Phipps
And
Cindy A. Phipps

This book is dedicated to students who are placed in groups

Acknowledgement

We wish to thank Britton Purtee, Matt Dickinson, Jason Phillips and Seth Spainhour for drawing the cartoons in this book

Table of Contents

INTRODUCTION 1

PART I - CONCEPTS 5

COOPERATIVE LEARNING 7
1. POSITIVE INTERDEPENDENCY 7
2. INDIVIDUAL AND GROUP ACCOUNTABILITY, AND PERSONAL RESPONSIBILITY 8
3. FACE TO FACE PROMOTIVE INTERACTION 8
4. INTERPERSONAL AND SMALL GROUP SKILLS 9
5. GROUP PROCESSING 9
CONCEPTS IN TEAM BUILDING 9
GROUP DEVELOPMENT 10
LEADERSHIP 11
CONFLICT AND COOPERATION 12
GROUP DYNAMICS 12
COMMUNICATION 13
TASK AND GROUP MAINTENANCE 14
EMOTIONAL ISSUES 14
COHESION BUILDING 15
OTHER DIRECTEDNESS 18

PART II - SKILLS AND ROLES 19

COMMUNICATION SKILLS 21
GIVING AND RECEIVING FEEDBACK 21
LISTENING ACTIVELY 22
CONFLICT STYLES 23
CONFLICT RESOLUTION 25
GROUP ROLES 26

PART III - TACTICS AND STRATEGIES 29

CONTRACTS 32
SETTING GROUP NORMS 33
THE PROCESS OF PROBLEM SOLVING 33
PERT CHART 41
PROCESSING 43
CELEBRATIONS 59

THE GROUP BOOK
Effective Skills for Cooperative Groups

Introduction

So you got put in a group again! Was your last group a good experience or something you don't want to repeat? Did you all pull together or did you have free riders? You might have been on-line with your project team and have been surprised at the sudden decline in civility. You probably ask, *"For goodness sake, why can't we just do individual work and get an individual grade?"* Several things might have sprung to mind for you when your instructor explained the group requirements for your course. *"Is this professor trying to get out of teaching by using group work?"* *"I've got good grades on my own in the past and the last thing I want is to have to rely on somebody else for a grade."* Of course, if you never have exactly been classed as an academic overachiever you might be thinking, *"Yes! I'll just get in that brainy-looking-kid-in-the-front-row's group and I'll be coasting."*

The truth is that preparation for classes using group work is usually more extensive for the instructors than if they simply prepared straight lectures for memorization. If you are a student looking for maximum learning, then you will want to know that much of the current thinking and research points to the fact that student learning is more effective done through cooperative learning techniques.

If you are looking for a free ride, you may find your group prepared to challenge you to be a functional group member and this may be the most rewarding class in your academic career.

Why are groups important?
- When functional, groups produce a better quality product (the key word here is *functional).*
- Being part of a team (as opposed to just a group) can be a very satisfying experience.
- You only learn functional group skills by practicing them -- in a group.

When you leave college and get into work situations, unless you are the Maytag repairman, you will be part of some kind of project **team,** committee, etc., (hopefully, not just a group). You will **not** be asked to sit at your own desk and not talk to anyone and be expected to just listen and memorize. **This will not happen.** You will be given a project and be expected to use all the resources you can to do the best job you can. Now this means using other people - - a group! *"Aaahh"!* You might say. But with the practice that you got in school and college, working cooperatively with your fellow classmates using this book, your group will progress to become a team!

Whew! Better to learn all those functional group skills now than on your first job.
Also, when you are asked the question, *"What kind of team player are you?"* at your job interview, you will be able to respond in detail and explain how teams are made and maintained because most people 'in the know' realize that they don't just happen. A team is trained and skilled.

What do I need to know about groups and teams?

There are endless books and tons of research on this topic, but we suggest for your work at school or college the following concepts and skills will get the cooperation and collaboration going, maintain it, and enable you to more enjoy your project teams.

Concepts

There are several concepts that need to be understood to enable high functioning teams. They are listed below, and explained more fully throughout this book.

Cooperative Learning is a method of learning in groups. It requires that you integrate five principles into your group work -- positive interdependency, face to face promotive interaction, individual accountability and personal responsibility, interpersonal and small group skills, and group processing.

Group development - - groups progress through stages to get to be a team.

Leadership - - everyone can exhibit leadership roles in the group; you are all going to be leaders pulling and pushing each other along using some definite skills and tactics. Leadership can be distributed amongst the group.

Cooperation and conflict are the two sides of the same coin - - one has to be learned with the other.

Group dynamics can be complex, but an understanding of group dynamics can remove the worries of what you might perceive to be "weird" behavior in groups.

"Other directedness" is a frame of mind enabling you to do what you can do for others. Everyone likes the "other directed" person and this can lead to promotion in the work place and definitely makes for effective team building and maintenance.

Skills and Roles

Communication skills, sometimes referred to as social skills or people skills, are what are required to move the group along to team status and keep it there.

Leadership skills are included here too, but we use a different definition than you may be familiar with. In Distributed Actions Leadership Theory, everyone is expected to keep the group moving forward by using facilitation skills. Roles that are practiced in the group can be either functional or dysfunctional. Everyone practicing the functional roles distributes the leadership skills around giving everyone responsibility for group building and group maintenance as well as tasks. Cohesive groups, where people in the group function well together don't just happen. Specific actions are usually necessary to build cohesion and eventually interdependence. Interdependence is where personal issues have been pretty much resolved and the group can function on the task at hand most efficiently, recognizing each other's strengths and weaknesses in non-judgmental ways. Also, the group will not stay cohesive without continued work on the group process to maintain this position. Keeping an eye out for dysfunctional behavior and confronting it helps maintain a positive communication climate.

Tactics and Strategies

A strategy would be to agree on using distributed leadership; tactics might include using techniques like:

- Establishing clear *goals* - - there might be different perceptions of what the goals of a project are, so clarifying this immediately is important.
- Setting *expected behaviors* in the group - - expected behaviors in a group are called group norms. You can set these at the outset by discussing the behaviors that you want to happen and ones that you prefer not to happen. Norms will emerge and if they happen to be undesirable, are usually more difficult to correct. In the case of norms, prevention is often easier than trying to change emergent behaviors. Professors and teachers can refer to more detailed information on this by reading the article, Group Norm Setting (Phipps and Phipps, 2003).
- Deciding on *consensus* rather than majority vote - - Roberts' Rules of Order have their place especially in committees that may include lots of politics and 'turf' issues. In such cases to make any kind of progress, voting is often necessary. In a project team, where the group is often together for a fixed amount of time and where creativity and ownership are more important, then cutting some group members out of decisions using a vote could be too divisive. Subsequently, reaching cohesion and interdependence would be difficult for the team. However, if a vote is not to be taken, then skills in mediation and conflict resolution become very important. If no one in your group can compromise, then you will not be able to move forward to be that high functioning cooperative group where the members are not only cohesive, but are interdependent. Don't forget that interdependency means that all the team members are working together using each other's

strengths while focusing on the task. This is done in such a way that the process is effective and enjoyable. Getting to this point requires practicing good group skills to enable all individuals to maintain ownership in the project.

- *Processing* refers to *how* the group is functioning. This is often neglected in groups as many groups focus only on the tasks needed to achieve the project goals. If, however, the process is neglected and relationships begin to deteriorate, then the task will quickly follow downhill. So you need to look at how you are working. What is going well? What can be improved? Make continual adjustments.

Decision-making and *problem solving* can be complex, so break the problems and decisions down to more simplified steps or divide the process of problem solving into different categories. This is especially important when you are trying to integrate critical thinking to fulfill your goals.

PERT method of planning - - PERT stands for Program Evaluation and Review Technique. It was developed to build nuclear submarines. Now your projects aren't that complex, but any project being tackled by a group is complex, so a simplified version of PERT can help you to plan the stages that you need to complete. It also helps the team process as you see the plan visually unfold and become aware of what steps, if not completed, would hold up the whole project.

The following workbook will explain the above concepts more fully and give work sheets to plan strategies to assist your group in its mission to accomplish the task you have been set. Use this workbook with your group to work out the strategy for your success. First let us start with getting an understanding of some group and team concepts. Read through parts I and II before you begin working on your strategies.

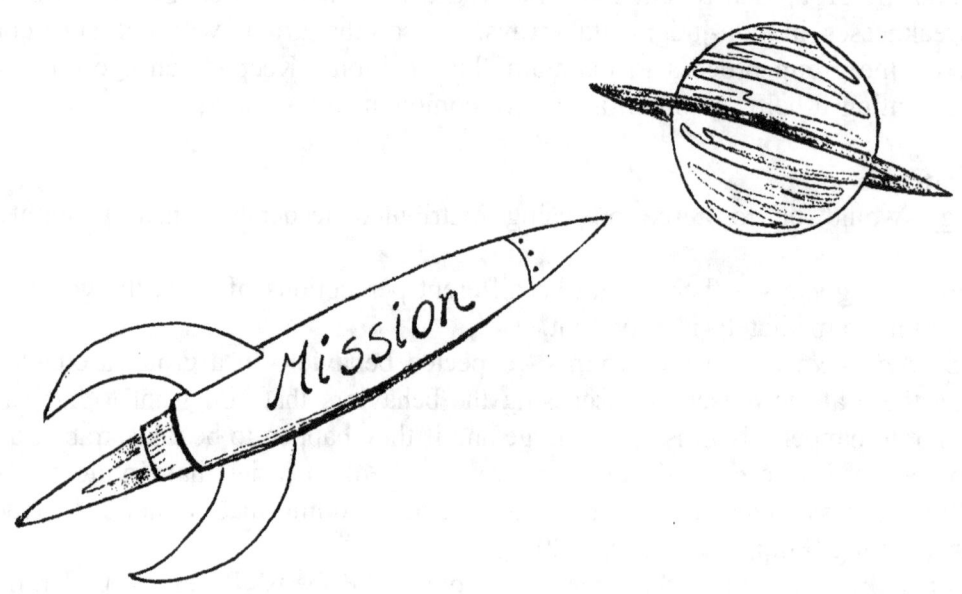

PART I
CONCEPTS

Part One: Concepts

Cooperative Learning

The underlying concept that we would like you to consider for your project team is Cooperative Learning. Your teachers might have structured the five elements of cooperative learning into the course that you are taking. As a group, you need to include these into your planning strategy and group norms. If you don't, then you could have "free riders", frustrating communication blocks, and a multitude of other problems. Johnson, Johnson and Holubec (1992), from the Cooperative Learning Center at the University of Minnesota describe the five elements of cooperative learning as follows:

1. Positive Interdependency

As a group you must believe that you will "sink or swim together." The perception must be that one cannot succeed unless everyone succeeds. Each person's efforts benefit all, creating a commitment to other people's success as well as one's own. This may require a real mind set change for the Internet Generation and general "scrappers." Remember the "other directedness" concept. If there is no positive interdependence, there is no cooperation. Positive interdependence is achieved by everyone committing to the group and the project - - and by sharing time, information, and effort as equally as possible.

2. Individual and Group Accountability, and Personal Responsibility

Each member must be accountable for contributing a fair share of the work and not "hitch hike." It includes assessing who needs extra assistance, support and encouragement. The truth is that as you provide instruction to a group member who needs it you "cement" your own knowledge. The purpose of using cooperative learning in groups is to help improve all the individuals in that group. A commitment is required to ensure that everyone contributes and understands all the material connected with the project.

3. Face to Face Promotive Interaction

Cooperative Learning groups are both personal and academic support groups. Through interpersonal interactions, cognitive learning is increased. Things like oral explanations, discussions, connections to other learning, testing each other, teaching each other all improve the learning. This fits nicely with the SQ3R method recommended for most effective studying.

Remember - - Survey, Question, Read, Recite, and Review. Often students without a group find it awkward or silly to recite material to themselves. Yet the actual recitation of the material can be a significant part of learning it. Personal commitment is increased as the group promotes this kind of work together.

4. Interpersonal and Small Group Skills

To get the task accomplished most effectively, groups must function as a team. This requires that all members practice good team skills, which includes effective leadership, decision making, trust building, communication, and conflict management. Everyone must also be *motivated* to use these skills. As a team member, try and think of creative ways that you can motivate your fellows. Strive to practice the team skills detailed in Section II.

5. Group Processing

Group processing includes discussing how the group is working. How effective are relationships? Are the goals being met and is the task being accomplished? How well? How can the group improve? Is the group standing by the group norms set by the group? What can you do when group norms are ignored or dysfunctional behavior happens?

For the group to be a high functioning cooperative learning group, **all** of the above five cooperative learning elements need to be included continually in the group strategy. If the group gets the motivation to build in all these elements, then a higher functioning team will grow with more student learning. The most difficult and often most neglected part of cooperative learning are elements 4 and 5. The teacher usually structures elements 1, 2, and 3 through various classroom strategies. Elements 4 and 5 are crucial; so the remainder of this book focuses on these elements - - small group skills and group processing.

Concepts in Team building

Groups often experience conflict. Feelings become intensified and incidents magnified. This is compounded by a lack of awareness on the part of group members in how their behaviors affect each other and a lack of understanding that **all** groups will experience conflict as part of normal group development.

Group Development

Groups go through an initial period where rules, roles, and rewards are all in flux. Cohesive groups are often noisy, they joke around, have disagreements or arguments and overrun time limits. Non-cohesive groups are often quiet, boring, and apathetic. They seldom disagree and deal quickly with important issues with little discussion.

Tension is always initially present and can be dealt with through smiles, laughs or jokes, or can be dissipated by humor, direct comment, or conciliation. Positive behaviors can be established by being supported and eventually becoming norms. Norms are the common beliefs of the group, which lead to expectations of behavior. They help interactions by specifying the responses that are expected. Norms are best formally established - - through discussion by all group members. This is not necessarily something we are naturally going to do, so it requires a savvy group member to orchestrate it. This could be you.

As groups develop, there is a human component, establishing and maintaining relations, and a task component, the job to be done. Anticipating the kinds of group interaction problems that are predictable enables better facilitation and choice of group role. As the stages of group development are predictable, they can be controlled. For example, good organization and use of distributed leadership skills (functional group roles) can ease the group through the conflict stage. The two dimensions (1) personal relations (interactions) and (2) task functions (what tasks are being done toward completing the project), combine at the different stages of group development. Four stages of development are suggested by Jones (1973) are summarized below.

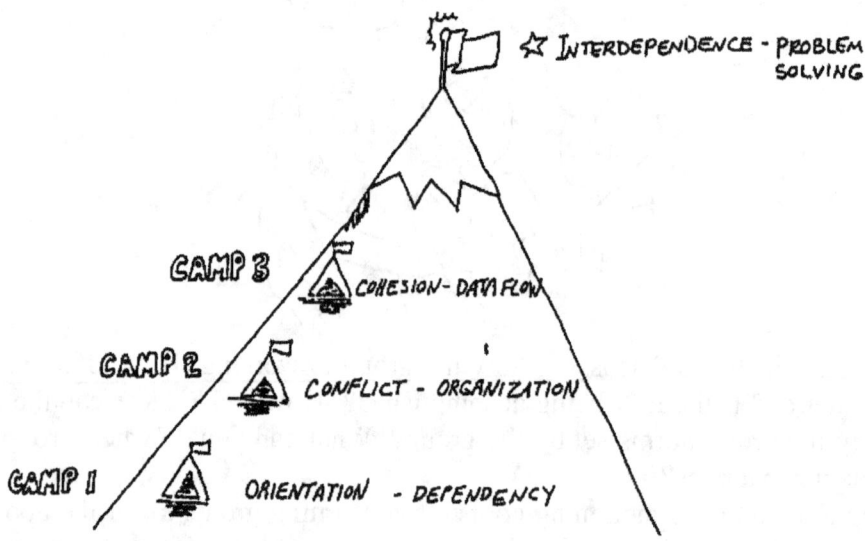

Initially, personal relations show dependency on the leader who sets the ground rules. At this stage the task function is orientation of individuals to the work involved. Individuals will be questioning why they are here, what they are going to do, how it will be done, what the goals will be, and possibly, how little they can get by with doing.

Next, conflict develops in personal relations, and organization emerges as a task function. The conflict may be covert but it is there. Conflicts are normal expectations. In fact, now that you anticipate there will be conflict, you can talk to your group about it before it happens, and plan for how to deal with it. Johnson and Johnson (1975, p. 231) suggested that, "It is not the presence of conflicts that cause disastrous and unfortunate things, it is the harmful and ineffective management of conflicts." Conflicts come from contention for leadership, task, influence and popularity. They are complicated by our own unresolved problems with authority, dependency and rules. At this stage the group has emerged through orientation and is feeling less dependent on the leader. A desire from the group emerges to organize both tasks and relationships that create conflict as different ideals clash. Here is where your planning and organizing skills will prove invaluable.

If the group resolves the interpersonal conflicts, a sense of being a team is achieved and the cohesion enables data-flow to take place efficiently. Ideas are shared along with feelings, and feedback is given. There is a sharing of information related to task, and people feel good about belonging to the group. There could be a period of play unrelated to the task, an enjoyment of the cohesion. Let the good times roll! Interdependence is not achieved by many groups. Read on for a description of what your group could be like! There is a high commitment to activities related to the common goals.

Experimentation with problem solving is supported and there is collaboration and competition that is functional. Members of the group can interact with each other as a team. They are more than cohesive, they have no fears in sharing points of view as they respect each other's expertise. Divergent thinking is accepted and encouraged within the group. The members are interdependent and not reliant on a specific leader unless the task changes to something unfamiliar. Doesn't interdependence sound worth striving for?

Understanding the developmental stages is useful as a predictor of group behavior. For example, if conflict is expected, then followers will be less anxious when the group starts to experience it.

Leadership

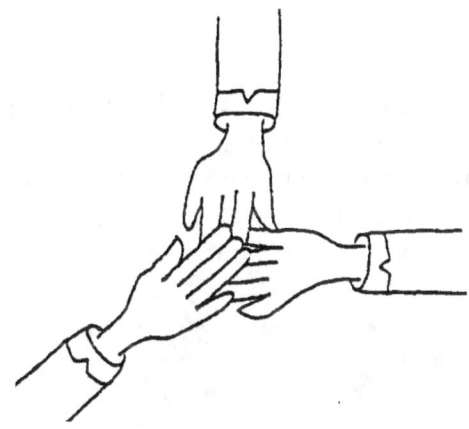

Everyone in the group can practice leadership skills (for details of these skills look under the Skills Section - -part II). Johnson, Johnson, and Holubec, (1992) suggested a Distributed Actions Theory of Leadership - - the idea is that anyone moving the group forward in the task or relationship using a positive group role is actually in a leadership role. Remember, interdependence means <u>not</u> relying on <u>one </u>leader. So you can all practice leadership skills by facilitating task behaviors, group building behaviors, and group maintenance behaviors.

Conflict and Cooperation

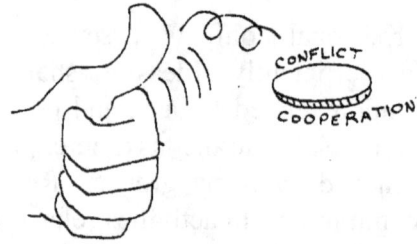

As we are trying to be cooperative in our intentions and as we know that conflict will arise and that this is a normal progression, then we need to understand the usefulness of conflict in learning situations and how to behave in conflict situations. Johnson, Johnson and Smith (1991, p 7:4) state, "Controversy increases the number of ideas, quality of ideas, creation of original ideas, the use of a wider range of ideas, originality of expression in problem solving, more creative solutions, more imaginative solutions, more novel solutions, and the use of more varied strategies." In some cases actually designating a "naysayer" or "devil's advocate" for a particular discussion can be a very positive step. For the skills required, see part II.

Group Dynamics
(Pfeiffer and Jones, 1973)

The group process is the dynamics of what is happening between group members while the group is working on the content or task. Process and content make up all interactions. The group process or "dynamics" is often neglected even when it causes serious problems. As it emerges, it encompasses morale, tone, atmosphere, influence, and participation, style of influence, leadership struggles, conflict, competition, and cooperation. Four areas of group dynamics that would be useful to understand are:

1. Communication
2. Task and group maintenance
3. Emotional issues
4. Cohesion building

Communication

   Without effective communication, a breakdown in the team will ensue. Communication includes getting the message across as intended, but also creating a receptive atmosphere, dealing with conflict, effecting motivation, and using good management techniques.   It is obvious that communication is essential, and taking the time to process your communication is equally important. Communication and participation are not necessarily the same.   Someone with little participation may still capture the attention of the group, while some may be verbose and ignored. Influence can be positive or negative; it can enlist support or alienate. You know the types of individuals we're talking about!

   Communicating feelings is as important as communicating facts. It should be a group norm to be able to express feelings and a good thing to own feelings and not make excuses for them. Refusal to include this kind of information reduces the individual's sense of worth and belonging – it de-motivates, causing bad morale. Expression of feelings may be inhibited, but non-verbal communication is often made through the tone of voice, facial expressions, gestures, etc. Active listening is often required involving showing empathy and doing perception checks by re-stating or paraphrasing (see part II skills). This creates trust and an understanding that anxieties are really being considered.

Task and Group Maintenance

To maintain harmonious working relationships and create a good working atmosphere, these functions are important as they move both the task functions and group relations forward. They include:
Gate keeping (helping others into a discussion or cutting off others)
Clarification of ideas
Evaluating suggestions
Diagnosing problems
Mediating arguments
Relieving tensions (by joking or placing the issue in perspective)
Celebrating good work that has been achieved.

The social aspects of the group involvement should not be underestimated, and the above suggestions help keep the group on an even keel. Group rewards such as pizza or other forms of celebration help instill cohesiveness and commitment to each other.

Emotional Issues

Emotional issues include power struggles, fears, identities, goals, needs, and intimacy. Dependency, fighting, and dominance issues can affect relationships and communication. For example, someone withdrawing emotionally affects the group, and pairing up can have negative consequences. Such issues need to be confronted either openly in front of the whole group or privately on an individual basis, depending on the situation.

Cohesion Building

If the group experiences relationship problems, explain that strong feelings and anger are acceptable, but use these tactics to deal with it:

a.   Stay in the here and now.
b.   Use "I" statements (e.g., I feel).
c.   Keep words congruent with feelings.
d.   Talk directly to group members rather than talk in general terms.

Make it clear that it is not necessary to justify personal feelings; have an expectation of no back stabbing and everyone model it.

Some techniques to enable cohesion are (Borman and Borman, 1990):

a.   Share stories, this promotes connectedness.
b.   Assign attainable goals
c.   When giving feedback to the group as a whole, give feedback as if the group is a person (see Part II – skills).
d.   Identify personal needs and either meet them or acknowledge the impossibility.

Develop cohesiveness by the following:

a.   Identify we, our, not they or me.
b.   Build a tradition through history, fantasy, and ceremony.
c.   Stress teamwork.
d.   Get the group to recognize good work.
e.   Give group rewards - - verbal, such as praising for meeting group norms; or food such as pizza, etc.
f.   Treat the group as people, not as machines. People have feelings. Always include time (group processing) for people to share their feelings, and make it an expectation rather than have people bury their problems.

An atmosphere is created in the way a group works. Individuals differ in the kind of atmosphere they like. Some prefer it to be congenial; others prefer conflict or competition. It can change from time to time from work, play, satisfaction and sluggishness to enthusiasm.

There can be an air of permissiveness, warmth, or defensiveness. People could be inhibited or spontaneous. The atmosphere is basically up to you as the group members. As you are all using leadership skills and roles, then you have some influence on this. Formally setting norms as a group early, then adhering to them (through regular processing) can also affect the atmosphere positively. An understanding of "defense mechanisms" in groups can help you to understand a group dynamic that alternatively can produce "fight" or "flight" interactions or manipulation of the group by members.

Defense Mechanisms in Groups (Thorenson, 1972)

Defense mechanisms are behaviors motivated by a personal need to maintain one's position in the group. Defense mechanisms evade conflict by moving away (flight) or toward (fight) the source of the conflict, according to Paul Thorenson (1972). His categorization of these defenses applies to any group as conflict often arises along with corresponding defenses.

Fight Defenses
1. Competition with the facilitator: This can be an attempt to build personal ego or avoid dealing with a personal problem.
2. Cynicism: This challenges the group goals through skeptical questioning of genuine behavior.
3. Interrogation: Someone giving heavy questioning may be trying to keep the spotlight away from himself/herself.

Flight Defenses
1. Intellectualization: This is a way of evading giving anything away personally or emotionally. It is sometimes done in introductions to avoid any self-disclosure. Self -disclosure done appropriately cultivates trust; intellectualizing evades giving personal or emotional information. Encouragement of "I" statements should help to discourage this.
2. Generalization: Impersonal statements about group behavior such as "we think" rather than "I think" means the individual may be speaking for the group without the group's consent.
3. Projection: One person's unconscious needs or behaviors projected onto another, he/she attributes to others traits that are unacceptable in him/herself (something one doesn't like about oneself that can be seen in another).
4. Rationalization: This is a substitution of less incriminating reasons to try and justify a decision, feeling, emotion, or statement rather than what is probably the correct one.
5. Withdrawal: Members suddenly falling silent are in flight. Individual confrontation followed possibly by group confrontation is necessary to bring such an individual back into the group.

Group Manipulation Defense
1. Pairing is sub-grouping to gain support.
2. "Red-crossing" is a defense of a person under fire to try and encourage mutual aid.
3. Focusing on one issue enables the group to spend excessive time on a person or issue to keep the action away from where it should be. Generally evasive maneuvering should be confronted using effective feedback techniques.

Another aspect of groups that will help you to achieve that cohesion and interdependence is the concept of creating and maintaining a positive communication climate. Jack Gibb (1961) suggested that the communication climate could develop to be either supportive or defensive.

Communication Climate (Gibb, 1961)

Creating defensiveness is the equivalent to throwing "mud in the works" as opposed to "oiling the machinery." A defensive climate is just much harder to work in, to communicate in, and to be a part of. Much more energy has to be spent to get the same amount of work done. Gibb defined defensive and supportive climates as follows.

A **defensive** climate is:

Evaluative - - the impression of not being good enough is given.
Person Control Oriented - - people are talked about a lot instead of problem solving.
Strategic - - deliberate attempts to distort and be calculating to effect "impression management."
Neutral - indifference is shown to the well being of people in the organization.
Superior Directed - - one-upmanship and putting each other down, discounting of others' ideas.
Dogmatic - - the need to be right all the time by individuals creates rigidity and inflexibility.

A **defensive climate** causes depersonalization, facade building, false role taking, strategic distortion, hostility, circumvention, aggression, and dependence.

A **supportive** climate is:

Descriptive - - people are non-judgmental.
Problem Control Oriented - - problem solving is the focus rather than people control.
Spontaneous - - there are no hidden agendas (ulterior motives) affecting behaviors.
Empathic - there is an expressed concern for the well-being of others. Support is communicated. There is a willingness to take the perspective of others.
Equally Directed - -There is mutual trust, and respect for each other is shown.
Egalitarian - - there is social equality.

Checking the Group Climate

Checking the group climate is part of processing and can be done using either of the two worksheets in the Tactics and Strategies Section. Worksheet X can be used to focus information for discussions on how support is being achieved or how defensiveness is caused.

Alternately, if you want to know in depth what is happening in the group and you wish to measure more accurately which aspects of the group dynamics are dysfunctional and why, then you could use the Group Dynamics Questionnaire (Worksheet XI).

The Group Dynamics Questionnaire (GDQ) was developed to measure group climate. The GDQ (Phipps, 1986, 1992) measures task and relationship functions as well as the following aspects of group dynamics:

Goals and Objectives
Communication, Atmosphere and Climate Participation
Group Interaction and Social Control Role Structure
Cohesiveness Leadership

After completion, the questionnaire can be just "eye-balled" for information, or statistically analyzed depending on how precise you want to get your information.

Other Directedness

Working as a team member sometimes requires sacrificing personal goals. Leaders who gain respect from group members are often the ones who are selfless and willing to support all members of the group. Added benefits to helping others include more "cognitive rehearsal" when concepts are explained and subsequently enable a better understanding and retention of material for the student doing the teaching. Students teaching students according to McKeachie, at al. (1986) is extremely effective for a wide range of goals, content, and students of different levels and personality.

PART II
SKILLS AND ROLES

PART II
SKILLS AND ROLES

Everyone in the group will need to practice certain skills and take on certain roles that help the functioning of the group besides the specific roles needed for different projects (such as word processor, editor, artist, etc.). The roles taken will lead the group to the ultimate goal and hopefully build and maintain the group as a team. Let's first look at communication skills.

Communication Skills

Giving and Receiving Feedback

When group norms are overstepped or problems occur, feedback has to be given for behavior to change. Feedback is the sending of clear messages back to someone in the group. When receiving feedback, individuals can become defensive but this can be overcome by giving feedback in as positive a manner as possible. Equate it as far as possible with "support." It is more easily accepted if the communication climate of the group is positive. Giving feedback requires accuracy, objectivity, and communication. Focus feedback on:

1. Behavior, rather than the person.
2. Observations, rather than inferences.
3. Description, rather than judgment; in terms of more or less, rather than either/or.
4. Behavior, related to a specific situation rather than abstractions.
5. Sharing of information and ideas, rather than giving advice.
6. Exploring alternatives, rather than giving answers.
7. The value it may have for the recipient, not the kudos or release for the giver.
8. The amount of information that the person or group can receive.

For example, if you said, *"You've been late to every one of these group meetings, and I'm tired of your laziness!"* you might end up with a black eye and a suspended group project. However, if you took this approach, *"I've noticed you've had trouble getting to our group meetings on time, and I'm concerned about our deadline for this project. Perhaps you could set the time for our next meeting at a time you know will work for you,"* you may see an upsurge in personal responsibility.

Using "I" messages we can communicate to group members what effect their negative or dysfunctional behavior is having on us specifically. This is different than speaking on behalf of the group. It goes like this:

<u>I feel</u>   (emotion)
<u>When you</u>   (behavior)
<u>Because</u>   (reason)

21

For example, "I feel very frustrated when you arrive late to our scheduled group meetings because we always have so much to accomplish and less time to use your skills to help us when you come late." As can be seen there is an art to using "I" statements in such a way that the offender who is being confronted is left feeling valued and subsequently could be more motivated.

In emotion labeling, we tentatively attempt to identify emotions we hear in the conversation of another person. "You sound somewhat annoyed. Is that what I'm hearing?" It's important to keep this tentative so the person has room to correct you. For example, *"You are angry,"* would be a judgment statement with no room for the person to correct you.

Give feedback at the right time and place. Excellent feedback presented at an inappropriate time may do more harm than good. For example if a person is angry and emotional, then it may be better to wait until he or she has calmed down. Attacking styles and non-constructive feedback need to be discouraged by using good communication skills to develop trust between group members so that they understand that feedback is part of the learning and communication process. Once trust develops and if the above guidelines are followed, feedback will be more readily accepted. Positive feedback is far more effective than criticism. The ability to inform people that they are wrong yet at the same time make them feel good is an incredibly valuable skill to gain.

Listening Actively

As the saying goes, it doesn't take a rocket scientist to recognize that "active" listening is distinguished by some specific actions. But some of us, whether we do rocket science or not, need to have those specific actions detailed because we don't all automatically do them. So what are we talking about?

1. Using varied eye contact with the group member who is speaking. A key word here is "varied." That's different from a long cold stare, which would of course defeat the purpose of the group relationship building.

2. Using natural relaxed and open body posture and gestures. Here again, this may seem obvious to some, but to the people who habitually cross their arms on their chest and lean back on the back two legs of their chairs at group meetings, breaking this little habit could make a big difference. Ever notice how talk show hosts lean in towards their interviewees and always use open hand gestures? The idea is to use your body to communicate your involvement.

3. Repeat key words, phrases, or sentences you've just heard. This is called reflecting and it nudges the conversation forward and keeps you, the listener, focused on the most important things the speaker is trying to communicate. For example, "I think that we need to revisit our group norms because there have been some infractions that we haven't addressed." Then you say, "We need to revisit our norms?"

Conflict Styles

We know from group development theory that conflict is going to appear even though you will have laid the group expectations by setting the group norms. Developing skills related to conflict promotes team building. It is essential to be able to discuss specific conflict behaviors in feedback and review sessions, so analysis of such strategies is needed. Describing and labeling conflict strategies enables recognition and helps considerably in conflict resolutions.

Conflict strategies should be viewed here as behaviors consciously chosen because of their importance to the individual.

Johnson (1996) gives the following conflict strategies:

1. **The Turtle**

Withdraws from conflict.

2. **The Shark**

Forces and tries to make other group members accept his/her solutions.

3. **The Teddy Bear**

Smooths and avoids the conflict in favor of harmony.

4.   **The Fox**

Compromises, giving up part of his/her goals and persuades others to give up part of theirs.

5.   **The Owl**

Views conflicts as problems to be solved, confronts, seeking solutions that will satisfy both parties.

Discuss Johnson's strategies above with all the class, making sure everyone understands that at different times, all of these styles are appropriate; however, judgment and thoughtfulness are necessary in choosing the appropriate style at the right time. The style chosen may be affected by the necessity to keep good relations, to do the right thing for the group goals, or achieve personal goals. Using the animal terminology to describe a group member's behavior can also be a less offensive, more playful way to make your point when the persistent use of one style is creating problems.

Conflict Resolution

NOT!

Johnson (1996) also gives detailed information on conflict resolution including defining the conflict, confronting, and negotiating. The skills that he suggests are:

1. Use of personal statements -- how the conflict affects "me."
2. Use of relationship statements --how the conflict affects us.
3. Use of behavior descriptions --behavior reference rather than personal attacks.
4. Direct descriptions -- be direct and to the point.
5. Understanding responses -- say how you understand explanations.
6. Interpretive responses -- inquire further if you don't understand responses.
7. A perception check -- give a summary of what you perceive.
8. Constructive feedback skills -- see earlier section on feedback skills.

Role-playing this sequence is an excellent way to practice it before the real event (and we know the real event will happen as a normal part of group development). Let us take a look at how this would work with a conflict between fictitious Fred and Fiona.

Fred: *"Fiona, you know, when you turn up late for our meetings, I feel let down."*

"I feel that it isn't helping our working relationship here." Behavior is referenced here in a way that is not attacking Fiona. It is direct and to the point.

Fiona: *"Fred, I'm sorry I am late again, but that old car of mine broke down again."*

Fred: *"So you are still having trouble with the car. Is it the same problem?"*

Fiona: *"No."*

Fred: *"Is it anything I can help out with?"*

Fiona: *"Not really - it needs a major overhaul."*

Fred: *"We are getting a late start on our project which can be a real problem for us getting inter-library loan material on time if we need it, but without transport for you we really have a problem."*

Fiona: *"Are there some alternative meeting times or places? What about meeting later? Then I can get a ride from my roommate if my car won't start."*
  Fred: *"That should solve the problem. Let's do that."*

Group Roles

Role functions in a group consist of the tasks needed to do the job and what it takes to strengthen and maintain the group. Roles emerge through the consistent use of certain behaviors. All these roles if applied functionally can be regarded as leadership roles if these actions move the group along in its willingness and ability to do the task (see page 49, Distributed Action Leadership Skills). **Educating the group about specific dysfunctional roles can eliminate unwanted behavior.** Jane Warters (1960) in *Group Guidance: Principles and Practice,* divided group roles into task, group building, group building and maintenance, and dysfunctional categories. She describes group roles as follows (illustrations are given by Fred, Fiona, and Ferdinand):

TASK ROLES
1. **Initiating activity**: solutions, new ideas, etc.
     Ferdinand: *"Would this be a good time to work out a time line for our project activities?"*
2. **Seeking opinions**: looking for an expression of feeling.
     Fred: *"Fiona, how do you feel about this?"*
3. **Seeking information**: clarification of values, suggestions and ideas.
     Fiona: *"Fred, in your experience, what would be a good way to approach this?"*
4. **Giving information**: offering facts, generalizations, relating one's own experience to the group problem.
     Fred: *"In my experience, it's best to start by doing a literature review."*
5. **Giving opinion**: concerns values, rather than fact.
     Fiona: *"I think that we should focus our literature review on employment opportunities."*
6. **Elaborating**: clarifying examples and proposals.
     Ferdinand: *"Since the job market is so competitive, focusing on employment opportunities will make it more useful for the students when we do our class presentation."*
7. **Coordinating:** showing relationships among various ideas or suggestions.
     Fred: *"Well, we can include the literature review in our PERT chart."*
8. **Summarizing**: pulling together related ideas and related suggestions.
     Fiona: *"We have a focus for our literature review and plan to do a PERT chart."*
9. **Testing feasibility**: making applications of suggestions to situations, examining practicality of ideas.
     Ferdinand: *"Do you think our topic is too broad-based on what was assigned?"*

GROUP-BUILDING ROLES
1. **Encouraging**: being friendly, warm, and responsive to others, praising others and their ideas.
     Fred: *"Fiona, I think you had a really good suggestion."*

2. **Gate keeping**: trying to make it possible for another member to make a contribution to the group.
     Fiona: *"Ferdinand, what aspect of the project appeals to you the most?"*

3. **Standard setting**: expressing standards for the group to use in choosing its content or procedures or in evaluating its decisions, reminding the group to avoid decisions that conflict with group standards (and norms).

Ferdinand: *"Coordinating the first draft -- as long as we stick to that group norm of everyone coming up with equal amounts of work toward it. Let's include time in our PERT chart for group editing afterwards".*

4. **Following:** going along with decisions of the group, thoughtfully accepting ideas of others.

Fiona: *"I think we should too because it will really improve our project."*

5. **Expressing group feeling**: summarizing what group feeling is sensed to be, describing reactions of the group to ideas.

Ferdinand: *"It sounds like there's some agreement about how much to include in the presentation. Should we look back at our goals?"*

BOTH GROUP-BUILDING AND MAINTENANCE ROLES

1. **Evaluating:** submitting group decisions or accomplishments to compare with group standards, measuring accomplishments against goals.

Fred: *"Does this presentation plan seem to be substantial enough? Do you think the class will get out of it what we intended?"*

2. **Diagnosing**: determining sources of difficulties, appropriate steps to take next, analyzing the main blocks to progress.

Fiona: *"If we don't meet earlier in the semester, we may run out of time as our other course work deadlines approach."*

3. **Testing for consensus**: tentatively asking for group opinions in order to find out if the group is reaching consensus.

Ferdinand: *"So, do we agree that this is how we will proceed with the project, or does anyone have another idea?"*

4. **Mediating**: harmonizing, conciliating differences in points of view, making compromise solutions

Fiona: *"Ferdinand, you have a good point but I think we can incorporate some of Fred's suggestions while maintaining our general focus."*

5. **Relieving tensions**: draining off negative feelings by joking or pouring oil on troubled waters, putting tense situations in a wider context.

Fred: *"There's nothing like a last minute computer glitch to bring out a group's resourcefulness."*

TYPES OF DYSFUNCTIONAL BEHAVIOR

This aspect of group roles is very important to recognize and understand as these roles can create a negative communication climate. These roles should be **discouraged.**

1. Being aggressive: working for status by criticizing or blaming others, showing hostility against the group or some individual, deflating the ego or status of others.
2. Blocking: interfering with the progress of the group by going off on a tangent, citing personal experiences unrelated to the problem, arguing too much on a point, rejecting ideas without consideration.
3. Self-confession: using the group as a sounding board, expressing personal, non- group-oriented feelings or points of view.
4. Competing: vying with others to produce the best ideas, talk the most, and play the most roles.
5. Seeking sympathy: trying to induce other group members to be sympathetic to one's problems or misfortunes, deploring one's own ideas to gain support.
6. Special pleading: introducing or supporting suggestions related to one's own pet concerns or philosophies, lobbying.
7. Horsing around: clowning, joking, mimicking, and disrupting the work of the group.
8. Seeking recognition: attempting to call attention to one's self by loud or excessive talking, extreme ideas, or unusual behavior.
9. Withdrawing: acting indifferent or passive, resorting to excessive formality, daydreaming, doodling, whispering to others, wandering from the subject.

Such negative behavior as the above could be regarded as a symptom that not all is well with the group's ability to satisfy individual needs. However each person may interpret behavior differently. Content and group conditions must also be taken into account. For example, there are times when some forms of aggression contribute positively by clearing the air and instilling energy into the group.

PART III
TACTICS AND STRATEGIES

TACTICS AND STRATEGIES

Establishing a clear goal

First establish the overall group goal --what is the task that has been set for your project? What are the boundaries? What do you have to do to earn an A+? Clarify all this immediately, and if there is any confusion after your discussion, then communicate with your teacher or professor to gain the clarification needed. Sub goals and a plan will then be needed.

The Project Team goal is

_____

_____

Sub goals are

_____

_____

_____

Contracts

Creating a Positive Communication Climate (after Gibb, 1961)

Contract to include the following behaviors in the group norms to enable supportiveness.

CONTRACT

We contract to be:

Descriptive in feedback, rather than **evaluative**

Problem control oriented, rather than **person control oriented**

Spontaneous, rather than **strategic**

Empathic, rather than **neutral**

Equally, directed rather than **superior directed**

Egalitarian, rather than **dogmatic**

Group members' signatures

1_____

2_____

3_____

4_____

5_____

6_____

But before we set off on the wrong foot and potential misunderstandings loom ahead, it is essential to establish a positive communication climate. The best way to do this is to set group norms. This means asking everyone in the group what behaviors they expect for this group.

Setting Group Norms

It's tougher to do it later after informal norms have developed, so establish them right away. Brainstorm what you would like to see under some of the headings as suggested by Petzoldt (1984): Individual-to-Individual Behavior; Individual to Group Behavior; and Group to Individual Behavior (some examples are given). One group norm to be discussed would be whether or not to use consensus, voting, or taking it in turns, to reach decisions. Although many committees use the democratic vote, reaching consensus includes the idea of ownership and so is often preferable in project teams.

WORK SHEET I

Group Norms

Individual to Individual	Individual to Group	Group to Individual
Give praise	*Be prepared*	*Bring everyone into the group*
No put downs	*Be on time to meetings*	*No scapegoats*

Initial here to show that you all agree to the group norms

_____   _____   _____   _____   _____   _____

The Process of Problem Solving

How will you get started on your project -- which basically is a problem or sequence of problems to solve? Neubert (1990) suggested the use of the word **PROCESS.** This can initiate the process of getting going by following a set procedure as follows:

P = Plan Make a plan together and do a PERT chart after you have worked out all the details (see PERT chart, p.41).

R = Roles Are there specific roles required like doing research of different parts to the project, word processing, editing, etc. - besides the group roles (building and maintenance).

O = Ownership Does everyone have ownership in the decisions that are being made?

C = Communication Are the different aspects of communication being dealt with? Are messages clear and are members sensitive to feelings? Is the communication climate and atmosphere positive?

E = Evaluate Are you evaluating as you go so you can reach the final goal at the pre- determined time? Is part of the project going to hold you up? What could go wrong? Do you need to change to a plan B?

S = Sensitivity Is everyone being sensitive in their communication of differences and feelings?

S = Synergy If all the above is achieved, then you will be working as a team with synergy.

WORKSHEET II (PROCESS)

Write in the specifics for each section

Plan	
Roles	
Ownership	All check here
Communication	
Evaluation	
Sensitivity	
Synergy	
Safety	

Notes

Steps in Problem Solving

As you embark on these strategies, you will see that you will be starting to make decisions. For more complex decisions you might want to consider the following steps:

1. Perceive the problem
2. Define the problem
3. Analyze the facts
4. Develop alternatives
5. Select an alternative
6. Implement the selected alternatives
7. Evaluate continuously

Worksheet III (Problem Solving)

Perceive the problem (s)

Define the problem(s)

Analyze the facts

Develop alternatives

Select an alternative

Implement the selected alternative(s)

Evaluate continuously

WORKSHEET IV
Some questions to answer regarding a decision

1. What is right about our decision?

_____

2. What could go wrong?

_____

3. What could cause this to go wrong?

_____

4. What preventative action can we take?

_____

5. What is our contingency plan?

_____

6. When will our alternative plan swing into action?

_____

7. Will it contribute to attainment of the stated goal or objectives?

_____

8. Is it feasible and capable of execution?

Problem Solving and Critical Thinking

If you are put in groups in the classroom and given a project, the expectation often is that you will engage in critical thinking to accomplish the task. **Don't accept the first thing that comes to mind.** Bransford and Stein (1993) suggested using the mnemonic IDEAL to integrate critical thinking into your problem solving. IDEAL then stands for

I =   **Identify** all the problems -- locate all of them then change them to opportunities using creative thinking.

D =   **Define** the goals -- are there alternate goals? Critically analyze whether the goal you are choosing really solves the problem. Think tangentially; there may be many ways to solve this problem you have. Brainstorm all the angles and come up with the best goals you can that will solve the problem.

E =   **Explore** possible strategies -- use diagrams, graphs, charts; break the problem into parts; work backwards, etc. Is specialized knowledge required? Learn about relevant conceptual tools for your project.

A =   **Anticipate** the outcomes and act -- try and evaluate the outcome of your strategies before the final outcome; for example, test strategies or worst case scenarios.

L =   **Look back** and learn - for example, your approach to studying.

WORKSHEET V(a)
PROBLEM SOLVING AND CRITICAL THINKING
T-Chart

Identify all of the Problems	How can you change these problems to be opportunities?

WORKSHEET V(b)
PROBLEM SOLVING AND CRITICAL THINKING

DEFINE	**EXPLORE**	**ANTICIPATE**
Give three goals for your task	Give three strategies and new information	Give three possible outcomes (+ & -)

1		
2		
3		

LOOKING BACK, what did you learn?

PERT Chart

PERT stands for Program Evaluation and Review Technique and is more sophisticated than a simple time line. First, tasks are brainstormed, put in the order that they need to be done, then assess what tasks could be done at the same time. After this, different times are calculated to do each task (see worksheet VI). Now draw horizontal time line stacking the things that can be done at the same time (see Fig. 1 below). Tasks that can be done at the same time can be stacked, but the length of time to accomplish each stage might be different; so the longest path or the 'critical path' needs to be found through the time line. A complex formula can be used with different estimations of each time slot for real accuracy - but for our purposes here, one estimation of time between each action, then adding these times between the tasks on the critical path will suffice.

Example brainstormed list for a research project

1. Do prospectus -- plan and outline of the research
2. Do literature search
3. Design the methodology
4. Design the instrument or find an appropriate one
5. Do a pilot -- collect some data and test the instrument for reliability and validity or appropriateness of the instrument
6. Collect data
7. Analyze the data
8. Write the literature review
9. Write the method
10. Write the results
11. Write the analysis of results
12. Edit all written work and check for accuracy in methodology and written communication

Now assess what components can be done at the same time - draw the PERT chart horizontally stacking components where you can. Use worksheet VI to help you get this far.

Figure 1. Example simplified PERT Chart

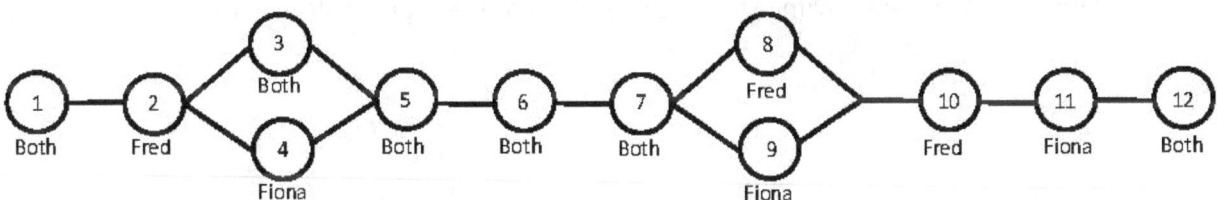

Completing the PERT chart after doing the critical thinking and brainstorming the "list" as a group makes it less likely that tasks will be forgotten. This works well for large groups. Writing peoples' names next to the set tasks creates a visual that shows where blocks to completion could happen if someone does not do his or her part on time and subsequently the project is held up. If everyone has a copy of this visual, or it is on a wall of a common office, then progress can be tracked along with times for task completion.

PERT WORKSHEET VI

1. Brainstorm all the tasks that need to be done to complete your project.

2. Put them in sequential order.

3. Stack the things that can be done at the same time

4. Draw out the events with "stackings" horizontally -- your PERT chart.

5. Work out the times (for greater accuracy this may mean contacting other people who have done a similar project). Add these to your chart above.

Processing

Processing is the time taken to look at the way your group is functioning. There are many ways to do this and a few ways will be given here. Creativity in processing is good to avoid the development of the attitude " here we go with the old processing again." It should be an expectation to discuss the process, and time must be set aside to do this regularly.

- Let's start with an easy question to ask your selves as a group -- "In looking at the way we worked today, what were two successful things and one thing that we could improve on the next time"?

- Sometimes the group might be inhibited in talking about the process, so the note in the hat exercise can reveal anxieties. Ask all the members of the group to write down their anxieties on a piece of paper anonymously and then drop them in a hat. The notes are then shuffled and each person in the group pulls out any note and reads it out aloud. The anxiety is then addressed by the group - - using good communication and good feedback techniques.

- Revisiting your group norms to check on how well you are living up to them is a good way to see your progress. One way is to ask everyone to go down all the items on the group norm list and rate each one with a 1-3 where 1 = not doing; 2 = sometimes doing; and 3 = doing most or all of the time. For any questions negatively phrased, the scoring would need to be reversed. Complete a chart as follows in Fig 2.

Figure 2.

	Mean Score	Comments
Be on time	2.8	Doing OK here
etc.	etc	etc.

See the next page for a work sheet on this.
- Using check sheets can pinpoint specific areas of the group process that need consideration; examples follow:
Revisiting Group Norms
"Other Directedness"
Observation of Distributed Leadership Skills
The Communication Climate
Group Dynamics
General Processing Questions Celebrations
Certificates

WORKSHEET VII (Processing)
Revisiting Group Norms

Group Norm	Mean Score	Comments
Example *Be on time*	*2.8*	*Doing ok here*

WORKSHEET VIII (a) (Processing)

Other Directedness Worksheet

Names_____

Group Members

Individual's actions ***Initials***	Person # 1	Person # 2	Person # 3	Person # 4	Person # 5	Person # 6
Gives compliments where appropriate						
Shows sensitivity to others						
Shares information and ideas						
Gives encouragement						
Shows commitment to group goals						
Accepts responsibility for task roles accepted						
Practices moving the group forward using distributed leadership						

Notes

Use this at an early session with one person acting as an observer and recorder. Checks can be made in each square for behaviors observed. This information can be shared amongst the group. These behaviors might seem foreign, so this exercise enables group members to practice them.

Use Worksheet VIII(b) at the end of the project to assess the behaviors. Assessing the behaviors could be done anonymously to gain more information that could summarize more accurately everyone's effort. Committing to do this at the outset will make it more likely that these behaviors will happen. The data will provide information by which you can process how everyone in the group perceived this aspect of the group process.

WORKSHEET VIII (b) (Processing)

Other Directedness Worksheet

Name of Group Member_____

Circle O, S, or N where   **O= Often**
S= Sometimes
N = Never

to reflect your perception of the above group member's actions.

Write specific examples in the spaces provided to enable feedback when you evaluate the group process.

Individual's actions	
Gives compliments where appropriate	O S N *Example*
Shows sensitivity to others	O S N *Example*
Shares information and ideas	O S N *Example*
Gives encouragement	O S N *Example*
Shows commitment to group goals	O S N *Example*
Accepts responsibility for task roles accepted	O S N *Example*
Practices moving the group forward using distributed leadership	O S N *Example*

Notes

Everyone in the group can anonymously complete one of these sheets on all the other members of the group. The subsequent information can then be used to process how you did as a group.

Remember that to reinforce these kinds of behaviors, everyone in the group needs to give continuous encouragement.

WORKSHEET IX Processing

Observation of Positive Group Roles after Waters (1960) (Distributed Leadership Skills)

After the group has been together for a short time, use the following check sheet to assess which roles are being used (refer back to pages 26 through 27 for explanations of these roles). Give specific examples of behaviors that you have seen so far with initials of participants who are beginning to take on these roles. Discuss what you are doing well and where you might improve.

Group Members
(Write initials in here)

_____

TASK ROLES

1. Initiating activity
2. Seeking opinions
3. Seeking information
4. Giving information
5. Giving opinion
6. Elaborating
7. Coordinating
8. Summarizing
9. Testing feasibility

GROUP-BUILDING ROLES

1. Encouraging
2. Gate keeping
3. Standard- setting
4. Following
5. Expressing Group feeling

BOTH GROUP-BUILDING AND MAINTENANCE ROLES

1. Evaluating
2. Diagnosing
3. Testing for consensus
4. Mediating
5. Relieving tensions

TYPES OF DYSFUNCTIONAL BEHAVIOR

Standard setting should help avoid the following negative group roles

Being aggressive
1. Blocking
3 Self-confession
4. Competing
5. Seeking sympathy
6. Special pleading

7. Horsing around
8. Seeking recognition
9. Withdrawing

WORKSHEET X (Processing)

Assessing Your Group Communication Climate (after Gibb, 1961)

Highlight where you think you are on the barometer and thermometer and check off the boxes that you think apply to your group at this time. Make notes on the specific actions and behaviors that you think are contributing to the defensiveness and/or supportiveness.

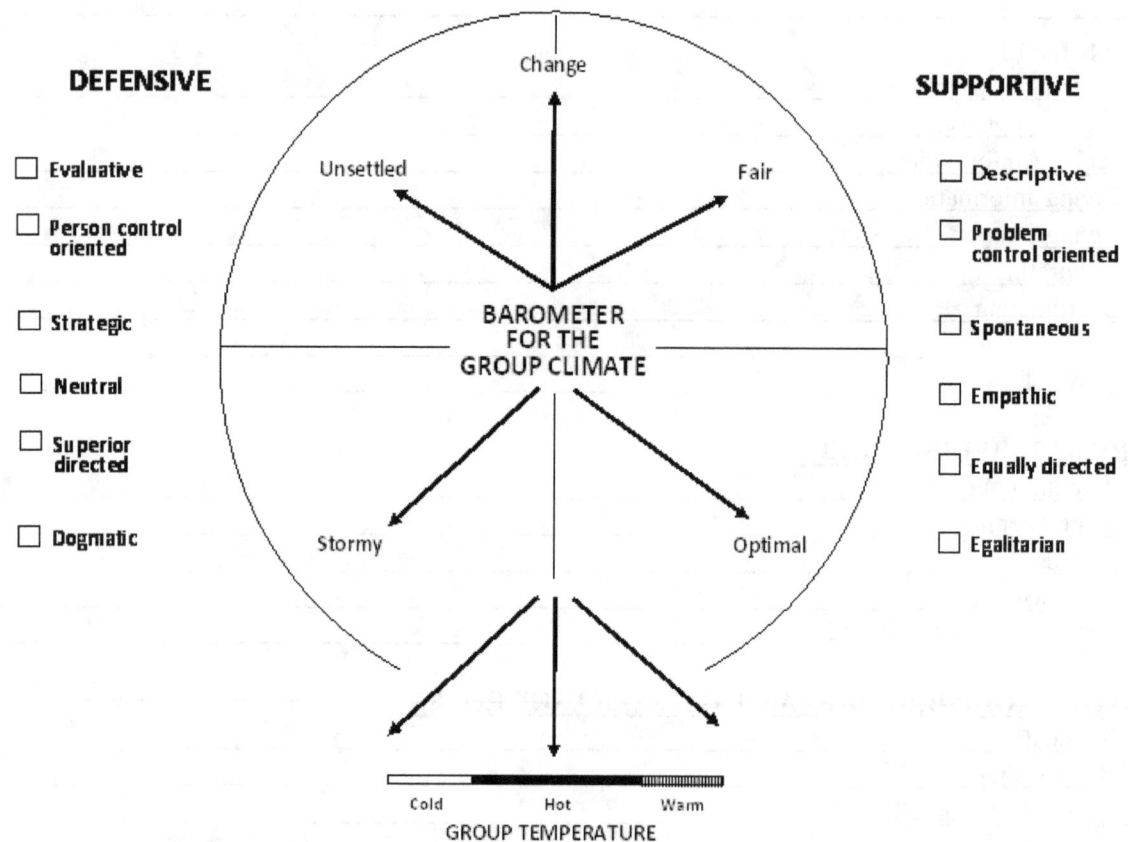

DEFENSIVE

☐ Evaluative

☐ Person control oriented

☐ Strategic

☐ Neutral

☐ Superior directed

☐ Dogmatic

SUPPORTIVE

☐ Descriptive

☐ Problem control oriented

☐ Spontaneous

☐ Empathic

☐ Equally directed

☐ Egalitarian

ACTIONS THAT ARE CAUSING DEFENSIVENESS

ACTIONS THAT ARE CAUSING SUPPORTIVENESS

WORK SHEET XI (Processing)

<u>THE GROUP DYNAMICS QUESTIONNAIRE</u>

Directions: Fill in column A the points which tell how true each of these statements is of the group. Add comments in column C

<u>If the statement is:</u>

Completely false..   1
False much of the time..   2
Sometimes true and sometimes false..................   3
True much of the time...   4
Completely true...   5

Column	A	B	C
Example: *There are too many group members* **GOALS AND OBJECTIVES**	5		*We have 30 members which decreases the personal interaction*
1. The goals are clearly defined			
2. There is definite recognition of present position in relation to goals			
3. Means and activities are instituted which will lead to goal attainment			
4. Means to goal attainment are cooperatively set			
5. Members are generally assigned to particular tasks			
6. Completing the day's tasks takes precedence over personal struggles			
7. Judgment is the top priority in decision making			
8. Uniform procedures are encouraged			
9. Scheduling is flexible			
10. The goals that were originally set are being met			
Communication, Atmosphere and Climate			
11. There is an air of permissiveness and warmth			
12. People are inhibited			
13. There are unresolved personal tensions			
14. All members communicate equally well with each other			
15. The members talk "Head talk"			
16. Sufficient information is given to complete set tasks			
17. Specific communication skills are dealt with in teaching situations			
18. The communication climate is personal control oriented (unnecessarily manipulative)			
19. Communication is spontaneous			
20. The members feel free to talk "Feeling talk"			

Participation			
21. All members contribute to the group process			
22. All members are assuming responsibility			
23. There is encouragement for all to participate			
24. Certain members consistently "get lost"			
Group interaction and Social Control			
25. Interaction patterns in the group are individual			
26. Interaction patterns in the group are cooperative			
27. Interaction patterns in the group are competitive			
28. There are hidden agendas			
29. Members conform to group norms			
30. Members are given recognition for meeting group norms			
Role Structure			
31. Members understand the nature of productive group member roles			
32. Members are engaged in both group task and group building roles			
Cohesiveness			
33. The group exhibits a definite "we" feeling			
34. Members demonstrate a common concern with regard to other members and the group as a whole			
35. Members understand that groups normally develop through a "conflict of interest" stage			
36. Members show a genuine willingness to work and sacrifice for group consensus and group goals			
37. Members regard the group and its activities as attractive			
Leadership			
38. There is a definite feeling that leadership is present			
39. Clear-cut decisions are made			
40. The members are accepting of the leadership style			
41. Group decisions that are made by the group are generally only changed by the group			
42. The decision making in the group is mainly leader centered			
43. The decision making in the group is mainly group centered			
44. The decision making in the group is determined mainly by the situation			
45. The style of leadership is effective			

Additional Comments

Questionnaire Directions (GDQ)

Filling out column C is extremely important for all group members to enable needed changes to be made. A more detailed explanation of the questions are as follows:

1. The goals of an organization are extremely important. Is everyone leading in the same direction? Have the goals been discussed?
2. Where is the group in relation to the goals; has this been made clear to the group?
3. Pertinent activities assist in reaching goals.
4. Members of the group participate in setting ways to reach the goals.
5. Members are given specific roles to assist in the task.
6. This could be positive or negative depending on the type of group/life-cycle/environment.
7. Is judgment used to make decisions, or are decisions made without much thought?
8. People are encouraged to follow similar procedures (standard operating procedures).
9. To what extent is the scheduling flexible or fixed?
10. Is the group heading toward the same goal, or has this changed? Has the original goal been forgotten?
11. The group climate is open, warm and supportive.
12. Members are not comfortable in saying what they feel.
13. There are some personal problems within the group interactions.
14. Members for the most part get on with each other in respect to communication.
15. Members talk "thinking" talk (intellectual talk).
16. Tasks seem to be organized clearly.
17. The leader uses definite communication techniques in teaching situations.
18. The leader tends to exert power unnecessarily over followers.
19. People feel free to act and speak when and how they feel without feeling inhibited.
20. Talking about feelings is acceptable in the group.
21. Do all group members contribute or are some members withdrawn?
22. Are some members not taking responsibility for tasks in the group?
23. Encouragement is given for participation to all e.g., compliments, verbal encouragement, group outings, get-togethers, etc. to include everyone.
24. Some members "space out" or withdraw from the group activities inappropriately.
25. People are expected to work on their own.
26. People are expected to work together.
27. There is more than friendly competitiveness between group members.
28. People have ulterior motives in the group.
29. People conform to expected behaviors.
30. Expected behaviors in the group are rewarded with some kind of recognition, e.g., positive comments.
31. There are positive roles in groups such as gatekeepers and group maintenance -- do members understand this kind of thing?
32. Members work towards building relationships as well as completing the tasks in the group.
33. Members of the group feel a sense of togetherness.
34. Everyone is helpful to the needs of others.
35. In all group development, one stage is a conflict stage. Does the group understand this?
36. The use of group consensus is important to develop cohesiveness rather than voting.

The Group Dynamics Questionnaire can be just "eyeballed" for information or if you wish to investigate the group dynamics in real depth to determine the group's perceptions on positive and negative functioning, then you can score it.

Scoring the Group Dynamics Questionnaire

	+2	(5)
	+1	(4)
Transpose the scores from 1-5 to	0	(3)
	-1	(2)
	-2	(1)

Transfer these to Score Sheet I on page 58 taking care to reverse the score where you see a shaded area (these questions are phrased negatively). For some groups other questions might also need to be reversed, but this depends on the type of climate expected in your group. Check all the questions in relation to whether they should be positive or negative before scoring.

Total the columns on Score Sheet I. This gives the raw score for each column. Divide by the total possible score for that column to give the % score. Do this for each column.

The task and relationship scores should be combined at the bottom left hand corner of the score sheet. Some questions referred to both task and relationship at the same time. To include all task and relationship scores, column A needs to be combined with column C and with column B. This affects statistical information in reference to separating task and relationship scores for the whole instrument because of the interaction of these scores when combined. Divide A + C (raw score) by 48 and A + B (raw scores) by 48 to obtain the % scores.

In the table on the score sheet, place your raw scores, % scores, and the mean % scores of the whole group for each sub-section of the questionnaire. The % scores for the whole group are calculated by adding the % scores for each person in the group on the different components (task, relationship, etc.), then dividing these totals by the number in the group who filled out the questionnaires (see Group Dynamics Score Sheet II). The individual and group % scores allow a comparison to see if a group member is out of sync with the rest of the group; this may mean the individual OR the rest of the group might be out of sync. For example, an individual might rate the communication, atmosphere and climate as -25% while the group rates the same subsection as +40%. This problem can then be addressed by looking at the comments on the questionnaire that qualify the numerical value given in the atmosphere section. It could be that the **individual** needs to change or it could be that **the rest of the group** needs to change.

It is essential that the comments are completed as fully as possible to enable the group to see what actually is causing the negative score. The group can then do something in regard to the problem which otherwise might have been buried by that person. If many of the scores are negative, then the group dynamics are negative and the comments should be studied to determine what areas need to dealt with. Scores will rarely be higher than 60% as it would be unusual to have everyone in the group give full positive scores for everything in the questionnaire. In general, scores 30% and above show a positive functioning group, 0 to 30% is actually positive functioning, but areas should definitely be looked at with a view to improvement.

Negative scores mean that something major needs to be done in those areas to improve the group dynamics.

The Group Dynamics Score Sheet's I and II can be found overleaf.

Group Dynamics Questionnaire Score Sheet I

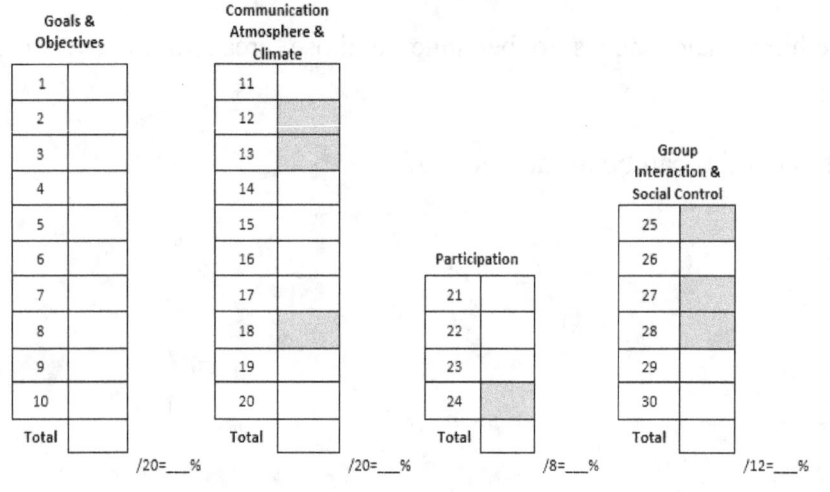

1. Convert 1-5 Likert Scale Points to +2 to -2.

2. Fill in the tables with 2, 1, 0, -1 or -2.

3. Reverse scores on shaded areas (negative phrased questions).

4. Add columns and write in totals.

5. Divide totals by maximum possible score to get a percentage.

6. Transfer percentage scores to the box below.

7. Work out mean scores of percentages of each person in the group and add these to the box below.

Goals & Objectives

1	
2	
3	
4	
5	
6	
7	
8	
9	
10	
Total	

/20=___%

Communication Atmosphere & Climate

11	
12	
13	
14	
15	
16	
17	
18	
19	
20	
Total	

/20=___%

Participation

21	
22	
23	
24	
Total	

/8=___%

Group Interaction & Social Control

25	
26	
27	
28	
29	
30	
Total	

/12=___%

Role Structure

31	
32	
Total	

/4=___%

Cohesiveness

33	
34	
35	
36	
37	
Total	

/10=___%

Leadership Components

38	
39	
40	
41	
42	
43	
44	
45	
Total	

/16=___%

Power

23	
18	
24	
40	
41	
42	
Total	

/12=___%

A

Task & Relationship Components

4	
17	
21	
22	
25	
26	
27	
20	
30	
32	
36	
37	
Total	

B

Relationship Components

11	
12	
13	
14	
19	
20	
26	
31	
33	
34	
35	
41	
Total	

C

Task Components

1	
2	
3	
5	
6	
7	
8	
9	
10	
15	
16	
39	
Total	

	% Scores	Mean % Scores
Total Task		
Total Relationship		
Leadership		
Power		
Goals & Objectives		
Communication, A & C		
Participation		
Group Interaction & Social Control		
Role Structure		
Cohesiveness		

TOTAL TASK = A + C _____ / 48 = _____%

TOTAL RELATIONSHIP = A + B _____ / 48 = _____%

Score Sheet II for the Group Dynamics Questionnaire

Calculation of the Mean Scores for
Participant's Perceptions of the Group Dynamics

	Person #1	Person #2	Person #3	Total	Mean
Total Task					
Total Relationship					
Leadership					
Power					
Goals & Objectives					
Communication, Atmosphere & Climate					
Participation					
Group Interaction & Social Control					
Role Structure					
Cohesiveness					

These mean scores can be transferred onto the table on Score Sheet I

WORKSHEET XII
(Processing)

General Processing Questions

1. Name one thing that you appreciate about each group member's contribution to the group. E.g., "You had some really good ideas!" Or... "I like how you encouraged others' participation!" Or, "You summarized our thoughts well!" Etc.

2. Ask each group member to finish this sentence:
One thing I could do to be a more effective group member, based on the group dynamics worksheet completed earlier, might be.....

3. Ask the group:
How did each of us contribute to our group's success today?

4. What is something that would help us improve our group's functioning?

WORKSHEET XIII

Celebrations

After completing sections of the work, finalizing specific goals and strategies, or resolution of some conflict, some kind of celebration is necessary. Use your imagination for *your* group. It could be a group cheer, hug (if in California), getting together for pizza or something else, but do celebrate your successes.

Ideas for your group

CERTIFICATE
FOR
PERSISTENT

COOPERATIVE EFFORT

TO _____

Reading up on more group and interpersonal concepts

This workbook was designed to help you through the process of a group project. The more you understand about how groups work, the more effective you will be as a group member or group leader. There is a mountain of information on groups. The authors of this workbook have been influenced in particularly by the following sources. We suggest further in-depth study using the following books:

Joining Together: Group Theory and Group Skills (11th Ed.) by David and Frank Johnson. Pearson, 2013.

Reaching Out: Interpersonal Effectiveness and Self-Actualization (11th Ed.) by David Johnson. Pearson, 2012.

The Nuts and Bolts of Cooperative learning (2nd Ed) by David Johnson, Roger Johnson, and Edythe Johnson Holubec. Interaction Book Company, 2007.

The Annual Handbook For Group Facilitators by J. Jones and W. Pfeiffer (Eds.). University Associates, La Jolla, CA.

Ideal Problem Solver by John Bransford and Barry Stein. W. H. Freeman and Company, 1993

Group Guidance: Principles and Practice by J. Waters, McGraw Hill.

Effective Small Group Communication (5th Ed.) by Ernest Borman, Burgess Publishing Company, 1996.

The authors especially would like to recommend the works of the Johnson family, which have had a tremendous impact on our work teaching in colleges and universities. This influence has been through David and Frank's writings on group work and interpersonal communication, David, Roger, and Edyth's writings on cooperative learning and Roger's encouragement and support as a mentor and teacher of cooperative learning through the University of Minnesota's Cooperative Learning Center summer institutes.

References

Borman, E., & Borman, N. (1990). *Effective small group communication.* (2nd Ed.). Minneapolis: Burgess Publishing Company.

Bransford, J., & Stein, B. (1993). *Ideal problem solver.* New York NY: W. H. Freeman and Company.

Gibb, J. R. (1961). Defensive communication. *Journal of Communication.* 11(3), 141-148.

Johnson, D. (1996). *Reaching out: Interpersonal effectiveness and self-actualization* (6th. Ed.). Needham Heights, MA: Allyn and Bacon.

Johnson, D. W., & Frank, P. (1982). *Joining together: Group theory and group skills* (6th. Ed.) Needham Heights, MA: Allyn and Bacon.

Johnson, D. W., Johnson, R., & Johnson H. E. (1992). *Advanced cooperative learning.* Edina, MN: Interaction Book Company.

Johnson, D. W., Johnson R., & Smith, K. (1991). *Active Learning: Cooperation in the college classroom.* Edina, MN: Interaction Book Company.

Jones, J. E. (1973). A model of group development. In J. E. Jones & J. W.Pfeiffer (Eds.). *The Annual Handbook for Group Facilitators.* La Jolla, CA: University Associates.

McKeachie, W. J. (1986). *Teaching tips: A guidebook for the beginning college teacher.* Lexington, Massachusetts: D. C. Heath and Company.

Nuebert, R. (1990). *The bulletin: Association of college unions international.* September.

Phipps, M. L. (1986). *An assessment of a systematic approach to teaching outdoor leadership in expedition settings.* Doctoral Dissertation, University of Minnesota.

Phipps, M. L. (1992). The group dynamics questionnaire. In D. Cockrell & K. Clement (Eds.).*The Proceedings of the Third Annual National Conference of the Wilderness Education Association at Pueblo.* Fort Collins CO: The Wilderness Education Association.

Phipps, M. L., & Phipps, C. A. (2003). Group norm setting. *Mountain Rise Electronic Journal.* 1 (1).

Thorenson P. (1972). Defense mechanisms in groups. In J. Jones & W. Pfeiffer, (Eds.). *The Annual Handbook For Group Facilitators.* La Jolla, CA: University Associates.

Warters, J. (1960).*Group guidance: Principles and practice.* New York: McGraw Hill.

Index

A

Active listening, 13, 22
Aggression, 17, 28
Atmosphere, 12, 13, 14, 16, 17, 34, 50, 54

C

Celebration, 14, 59
Circumvention, 17
Cognitive Rehearsal, 18
Cohesion, 3, 11, 12, 15, 17
Communication, 3, 7, 9, 12, 13, 14, 17, 21, 22, 28, 32, 33, 34, 35, 41, 43, 48, 50, 53, 54, 63
Communication Climate, 3, 17, 21, 28, 32, 33, 34, 43, 48, 50
Conflict, 2, 3, 9, 10, 11, 12, 13, 16, 23, 25, 27, 51, 53, 59
Conflict Resolution, 3, 23, 25
Conflict Styles, 23
Consensus, 3, 27, 33, 47, 51, 53
Cooperative Learning, iii, 1, 2, 7, 8, 9, 63
Critical Thinking, 4, 38, 41

D

Decision-Making, 9, 50, 51
Defenses Mechanisms, 16
Defensive Climate, 17
Dependence, 17
Depersonalization, 17
Distributed Actions Leadership, 3
Divergent Thinking, 11
Dysfunctional Behavior, 3, 9, 21

E

Emotional Issues, 14

F

Façade Building, 17
Face To Face Promotive Interactions, 2
False Role Taking, 17
Feedback, 11, 15, 16, 21, 22, 23, 25, 43, 46
Fight And Flight, 16

G

Gatekeeping, 53
Generalization, 16
Goals, 3, 4, 9, 10, 11, 14, 15, 16, 17, 18, 24, 27, 31, 38, 45, 46, 50, 51, 53, 59
Group Development-, 9, 10, 23, 25, 53
Group Dynamics, 2, 12, 17, 43, 54, 55, 57
Group Dynamics Questionnaire, 17, 54, 56, 57

Group Maintenance, 3, 11, 12, 14, 53
Group Norms, 3, 7, 9, 15, 21, 22, 23, 32, 33, 43, 44, 51
Group Processing, 2, 9, 15

I

Individual Accountability, 2
Interdependency, 3

L

Leadership, 2, 3, 9, 10, 11, 12, 16, 17, 26, 43, 45, 46, 47, 51

M

Manipulation, 16

N

Norms, 3, 9, 10, 16, 22, 27, 33

O

Other Directedness, 7, 18, 43, 45, 46

P

Positive Interdependency, 2, 7
Problem Solving, 4, 11, 12, 17, 34, 36, 38
Process, 3, 4, 12, 13, 22, 34, 43, 45, 46, 51, 63
Processing, 4, 9, 16, 17, 34, 42, 43, 44, 45, 46, 48, 49, 58
Projection, 16

R

Rationalization, 16
Red Crossing, 16
Reflecting, 22
Roberts Rules Of Order, 3
Roles, 2, 3, 10, 16, 21, 26, 28, 34, 35, 47, 51, 53

S

Small Group Skills, 2, 9
Strategic Distortion, 17
Supportive Climate, 17

T

Task Roles, 45, 46

W

Withdrawal From Conflict, 23